I0843486

DIVERSE LOVE

Revised Edition

Sharon Downey

2010 forward by Mr. Stephen Biddle

2025 forward by Mr. Johnny Depp (BEATS 2022 Poetry Laureate)

ISBN: 978-1-967361-79-3 (sc)
ISBN: 978-1-967361-80-9 (e)

Rev. date: 12/10/2025

CONTENTS

DEDICATION

Collection 2010 is dedicated to my late wonderful Grandmother Lilian, my late Grandfather John and to my amazing late Uncle Glenn.

At the time of writing the 2010 collection, my grandmother Lilian was still alive. Sadly, since then she has passed away at the tender young age of 92.

Collection 2025 is dedicated to the loving memory of my beloved mother: Wendy, who sadly, passed away in 2023. Without her, publishing my poetry to begin with back in 2010, would never have been possible.

2025 collection is also dedicated to my cuddly teddy elephant Johnnyphant, who has put up with my creative frustrations and encouraged me to believe in myself and to remain strong. By just being there to listen and let me think.

I also dedicate this entire book to my wonderful Dad, Michael.

Who has encouraged me and believed in me enough. To give it another go. Giving that loving support. Telling me, my 'Mother' in Heaven is shining down with her loving support.

ACKNOWLEDGEMENT

I wish to thank my good friend Elo designer or www.elodesigners.com for graphically designing the cover of Diverse Love for me.

For the images for 2010 collection poetry, I thank St Roo from Saintroo.com for creating such fantastic images.

I also wish to thank my good friend Stephen Biddle for providing the 'Forward' with kind courtesy allowing me to use his Black and White photo of himself. Fellow poet from England.

I like to thank good friend Alex Roamlyn (Alex White) from Roamlyn Media on Facebook for the kind courtesy use of his photo as his character: Captain Jack White inspired by Captain Jack Sparrow. For the poem 'Pirates'.

Alex Roamlyn / Roamlyn Media is based in Saint Augustine, Florida, USA.

Captain Jack White from 'Run With Jack' on his YouTube Channel, Facebook & Instagram.

I also wish to thank Servando Enrique Leira Quiros from the Boy Band PROVIDENCE for giving his permission by Courtesy to use his Black and White photo to accompany the poem 'Servando'.

I also like to thank Photographer Aaron Jenkins for the courtesy permission to use his photo of the Moon over St Michal's Mount.

To accompany my poem 'Lovers Blushers Moon'.

You can purchase his prints from Aaron Jenkins Photography via Facebook, Instagram.

For the poem 'A Poetic Letter to Johnny Depp' I like to thank Mr Johnny Depp for the courtesy use of using (Him by me) painted by Mr Johnny Depp. I purchased my print from 'A Bunch of Stuff' website through NFT: Never Fear Truth link.

For the poem 'Love Lives on' which is dedicated especially to Chris Fleming (Artist & Psychic Medium) and Ryan O'Neill (Scooby Doo) from Haunted Scotland Team (Haunted/Spooky Scotland/Ireland)

The photograph was taken by Ryan O'Neill and permission to be used courtesy from himself.

**(ONLY IF PERMISSION IS GIVEN)

Black and white photo of Mr Johnny Depp comes courtesy of Photographer Mr Ross Halfin, taken at the Jeff Beck Exhibition at London's Christie in January 2025. Anyone wishing to purchase a print can contact www.rosshalfin.com/

Author's photograph taken by Lavina
www.inspirestudios.com

Author's Makeup by Olga
For www.inspirestudios.com

2010 Collection Forward
By poet & musician Stephen Biddle

Some people are born to be a poet. Every poet has a love poem or two.

Miss Downey's poetry not only graces the imagination with sunsets of the heart and dawns of perpetually 'Deep Oceans'.

Her words are woven to invoke, your own journey as you journey with Miss Downey's - 'Rhythm and Rhyme'. Her effortless pros and verse.

The descent of pain. The joy of friendship. The vibrant colours of wisdom painted within her words.

The modern landscape breached as the past lives between Miss Downey's lines.

This lady's poetry captured in 'Diverse Love' is a must of contemporary and modern poetry.

A true Masterpiece bearing no disguise.

AUTHOR'S MESSAGE TO READERS

I hope the poems in this book will bring awareness to the diverse ways that love does indeed touch each and everyone.

With love, it could be possible that the world can achieve peace and harmony.

That the future generations can live in a better world. The power of words can make a positive difference towards the greater good.

You will notice how the collection of poems in 2010 are simpler; compared to perplexed or complex poems in the 2025 collection.

Simply because the 2010 collection was mainly typed in hospital. Quite often with one finger after a life changing situation. Most often my poems are written from my bed or sitting on the sofa.

I suffered multiple organ failure leading to two coma situations. I also 'Flat Lined' on four occasions. Leading to 14 T.I.A situations. I also had 4 tracheotomy Stenosis creating a bottle neck windpipe.

This led to major complications leaving with 'Muscular Skeletal Disorder,' & 'Muscle Fatigue.'

Several times I thought about giving up on my poetry. Like, what is the point? My hand cramps up. I can barely hold a pen at times and after typing, that to causes cramps. Plus, eye fatigue.

The point is - do not give up. Never, never ever give up.

Self-determination and dedication are also a form of love. Self – love.

Most important of all, it is not an act of selfishness - but love towards oneself. To focus on what we can do, rather than on what we cannot do.

The medical world and political world will class it as a 'Disability.'

However, my best friend in the world told me to think and believe that I am 'Perfectly Imperfect, Original and Uniquely Authentic as I am.'

If you acknowledge and accept what you can do. You will grow, your self-esteem, your confidence. Never, never ever quit!!!

- ***For the poems 'Love Eternal' and 'Love lives on' please be advised this is for reading entertainment only.***

Sharon Downey.

DIVERSE LOVE

REVISED

Collection 2010

MARRIAGE AS A CARIBBEAN ISLAND

LIFE IS VERY MUCH LIKE THE WEATHER,
MARRIAGE IS VERY MUCH LIKE A CARIBBEAN ISLAND,
THE EARTH AND IT'S WEATHER ARE UNPREDICATABLE,
VERY MUCH LIKE ALL LIFE UPON EARTH.

THE CARIBBEAN IS MADE OF MANY,
LITTLE ISLANDS.
WITH A DIVERSE RANGE OF LIFE,
THE MOST DIVERSE, I HEAR IS PUERTO RICO.

SORT OF LIKE LONDON,
ONLY TAKEN OUT OF ENGLAND AND BEING AN ISLAND.
MANY WAYS AND CULTURES, VAST TRADITIONS,
HOTTER, AND NOT AS OLD.

WE ALL HAVE OUR FAIR SHARE
OF BEAUTIFUL LANDS AND MODEL BUILDINGS.
WE ALSO HAVE THE HURRICANES AND RAINS AS WELL.
SO, WE ARE NOT THAT DIFFFERENT, REALLY.

WHEN I THINK OF MARRIAGE, I THINK OF IT
AS A CARIBBEAN ISLAND OR PUERTO RICO.
IF YOU IMAGINE THE WOMAN AT THE ISLAND,
AND THEN THE MAN AS THE WEATHER,
SOMETIMES, IT'S BLISSFUL AND OTHERS STORMY.

WHEN A STORM HITS THESE ISLANDS,
COMMUNITIES SEEK OUT SANCTUARY,
IT MEDITATES AS THE STORM PASSES.
THEN LIFE CONTINUES AND ALL IS WELL AGAIN.

WISH MEN AND WOMEN COULD DO THAT.
EVERY NOW AND THEN A LITTLE STORM
DOES DEVELOP INTO A MIGHTY HURRICANE,
BREAKING DOWN MANY BUILDINGS AS WELL AS LAND.

YET SOMEHOW THE LOVE OF THE
COMMUNITY IS ALWAYS THERE.

YES, THERE IS MUCH DAMAGE AND PAIN, YOU COULD
STAND THERE FOREVER, SHOUTING THE ODDS
IT WON'T GET YOU ANYWHERE,
SO, THEY COME TOGETHER.

OBSERVE, TALK, EVALUATE AND WORK
TOGETHER THE PEOPLE UNITE AND WORK
REMEMBER, THE LOVE AND BEAUTY.
THEY REBUILD AND RE-STORE,
ALL IS GOOD ONCE MORE.

SO, WHEN A MAN AND A WOMAN
COMES TO BLOWS, RUNNING HOT AND
COLD, LIKE TRADE WINDS EMOTIONAL AND
IRRATIONAL, THE LAST THING THEY SHOULD
DO, IS ADD FUEL TO THE FIRE, BUT THEY DO!

MORE THAN HALF THE TIME, WE ARGUE OVER LITTLE
PETTY THINGS THAT CAN EASILY BE EXPLAINED. IF
ONLY WE HAVE STEPPED ASIDE AND MEDITATED,
CALMED DOWN AND JOINED TOGETHER.

COMMUNICATE COOL AND RATIONALLY.

HALF THE TIME, STORMS COME,
FOR WE DON'T COUMMUNICATE PROPERLY.
LISTEN, OBSERVE, THEN WALK AWAY. RETURN
WHEN THE STROM HAS PASSED.

THE SEAS OF THE HEART HAS MELLOWED.

HAVE THEY HAD A BAD DAY?
WAS WORK HORRID?
WAS SOMEONE HURT?
WERE THEY STUCK IN TRAFFIC?

NOT START WITH,
WHERE? WHAT? WHO?
WHEN? TRY, WHY?
THEN, WHAT HAPPENED?

OFFER COMPASSION AND UNDERSTANDING,
NO FIFTY-FIFTY QUESTIONS, LIKE THE POLICE.
NOTICE THEIR ACTIONS, IS THIS NORMAL?
IF NOT, MAYBE SOMETHING WENT WRONG,
AND JUMPING IS, NOT GOING TO SOLVE IT.

TREAT A MARRIAGE AS IF IT WAS A TROPICAL
STORM, SEEK SHELTER AND WEATHER IT OUT.
ONCE THE ANGER AND PAIN AS PASSED,
FIND YOUR LOVED ONE AND TALK RATIONALLY.

OBSERVE THE DAMAGE, JOIN TOGETHER.
RE-BUILD THE FAMILY HOME,
IF THE WEATHER CAN GIVE TESTS, AND WE RE-BUILD,
THEN SURELY SOMETHING WE DID CAN BE RESOLVED.

WORDS ARE JUST PIECES OF WOOD,
SCATTERED BY THE STORM.
NO ONE IS PHYSICALLY INJURED,
NO DAMAGE OR DEATH.

YOUR COMMUNITY IS YOUR HOME.

YOUR FAMILY IS YOUR HOME,
YOUR MARRIAGE IS YOUR CARIBBEAN PARADISE.
IT'S LOVING, ROMANTIC, PASSIONATE, HOT OR SEXY.
JUST LIKE A CARIBBEAN ISLAND.

YOUR MARRIAGE ALSO HAS PERILS,
DROUGHTS, FLOODS, HURRICANES.
IT'S CALLED EMOTIONS.

THIS IS LOVE!
THIS IS BEAUTY!
THIS IS PARADISE!

IT TAKES EXTREME CASES FOR A COMMUNITY TO
RELOCATE, FOR THE DAMAGE IS TOO FAR GONE.
IN THAT CASE, WALK AWAY AND STAY AWAY, IN
THE NAME OF LOVE, PEACE AND HARMONY.

THERE ARE TIMES OF ABUSE...
EVEN THE WEATHER DOES THAT.

BEFORE YOU PACK A BAG, THINK ABOUT
IT. WHAT KIND OF STORM ARE YOU
FACING? BEFORE YOU GO FOR GOOD?
A RAIN CLOUD, A GALE FORCE, OR A HURRICANE?

NO ONE LIVES WHERE THERE IS ABUSE OR
DANGER. PEOPLE RUN FROM HURRICANES,
BUT NOT FROM RAIN CLOUDS!

THERE WAS A TIME LONG AGO

THERE WAS A TIME LONG AGO,
WHEN THINGS WERE HAPPY AND SIMPLE,
A WORLD,
THERE WAS A TIME LONG AGO.
WHEN HUMANKIND LIVED, LIVED AS ONE.
NO RACE, NO CREED OR RELIGION.

THERE WAS A TIME LONG AGO
WE LOVED UNDER ONE TRUE LAW.
THE GOOD; DEFEATING THE EVIL,
THE STRONG PROTECTING THE WEAK.

THERE WAS A TIME LONG AGO
WHEN PEOPLE LIVED OF THE LAND.
THE FRUITS, VEGETABLES AND GRAINS.
WITH FISH AND MEATS ALIKE.

THERE WAS A TIME LONG AGO
WHEN HUMANKIND AND ANIMAL KIND,
LIVED IN HARMONY.
ALONG WITH THE ANIMAS OF THE SKY AND SEA.

THERE WAS A TIME LONG AGO
WHERE THERE WERE NO TALL BUILDINGS,
THERE WERE NO COMPUTERS,

OR SKY TELEVISION.

THERE WAS A TIME LONG AGO
WHERE THERE WAS JUST YOU AND ME,
HAND IN HAND, EYES TO EYES,
LIPS TO LIPS.

THERE WAS A TIME LONG AGO
TWO WORLDS LIVED AS ONE.
THE MOON AND THE EARTH
FUSED AS ONE...

THE YIN AND THE YANG,
THE WARRIOR AND THE ANGEL,
THE DEFENDER AND HARMONY MAKER,
TOGETHER THROUGH TIME AND SPACE...

THERE WAS A TIME LONG AGO
WHERE BEINGS HAD NO FLESH,
NO BLOOD, TWO ENERGIES,

ACTIVE AND PASSIVE.

THE UNKNOWN ADVENTURE

AFTER A HARD DAY'S WORK,
HE SAT DOWN WITH A CUP OF COFFEE,
TURNED ON THE SIDE LAMP,
OPENED HIS BOOK TO READ.

WITH THE SOUNDS,
GENTLE SOUNDS OF PANPIPES.
IN THE BACKGROUND,
THE LIGHTS TUNRED LOW.

THE YOUNG ADVENTURER
BEGAN TO RELAX,
UNWIND FREE OF THE DAY'S TENSION.
WITH HIS DOG AT HIS FEET.

THE SOUND OF RAIN FALLING
AGAINST THE WINDOW,
THE SOUND OF WOOD
CRACKLING ON THE FIRE.

THE LONELY ADVENTURER
LIVING ALONE,
ALL ALONE,
ON THE ONE DAY HE WISHED NOT.

BOOKS EVERYWHERE,
PAPERS EVRYWHERE,
MUSIC EVERYWHERE,
HIS INNER DREAM? NOWHERE!

RESTLESS WAS HIS MIND.
HE NEEDED TO REACH OUT,
JUST ONE LAST GLANCE,
TO READ HER MIND, HEART AND SOUL.

THE SECRET ADVENTURER,
SO, SECRET HE HAD NOT SEEN.
WAS IT A MEMORY FROM HIS PAST?
WAS IT HIS HEART'S WISHFUL THINKING?

HE FELT CONNECTED,
FELT HER NEARBY,
WITH HER WORDS
FLOWING FROM HIS MIND.

THE TENSIONS
FREED FROM HIS MANLY SHOULDERS.
SIP OF COFFEE,
A SIGH OF RELIEF.

HE STARTED TO READ,
READ HIS BOOK, HIS FACE
GOT A CHAPTER IN,
FELL FAST ASLEEP.

'HAPPY BIRTHDAY, HANDSOME!'
SAID A SOFT WARM VOICE,

ASLEEP DREAMING,
DREAMING HIS SECRET ADVENTURE.

THE ADVENTURE OF THE HEART,
WITH HIS EYES CLOSED,
A GENTLE BOYISH SMILE
UPON HIS FACE AS HIS BOOK FELL FREE.

THE SMELL OF COCO CHANNEL,
THE TOUCH OF HER HAND,
AGAINST HIS HAIR,
HERBAL ESSENCE ALL AROUND.

HE STIRRED,
AS HIS IMAGINATION.
PLANTED A GENTLE KISS,
UPON HIS LIPS.

THE SOUND OF A PHONE
AWOKE HIM FROM HIS DREAM.
BUT WAIT, NOT THE PHONE,
FOR IT WAS HIS DOOR.

HE OPEND HIS DOOR.
TO HIS SURPRISE,
IT WAS HER, HE SAID NOT A WORD,
STEPPED FORWARD AND KISSED HER.

SUDDENLY,
IT FELT COLD.
HE HAS SPILT HIS COFFEE,
WAKING HIS REALITY.

NOW HE WILL NEVER KNOW,
WHAT NATURE HAD INTENDED.
COULD IT HAVE HAPPENED?
OR NOT?

AH, THE UNKNOWN ADVETNURE!

TO MY MUM

TO MY MUM,
I LOVE YOU SO MUCH,
MORE THAN YESTERDAY,
BUT LESS THAN TOMORROW.

I HAVE NO IDEA,
WHERE I WOULD BE?
WHAT I WOULD BE?
WITHOUT YOU.

I LOVE YOU MUM,
FOR YOU WERE THERE.
WHEN ALL HAVE GIVEN ME UP FOR DEAD.
NOT A NURSE OR A DOCTOR HAD YOUR FAITH.

WHEN MY HAIR FELL OUT,
YOU SAID IT WILL GROW BACK.
WHEN I WAS IN A COMA,
YOU NEVER GAVE UP.

WHEN I COULD NOT WALK,
WITH A BAD BACK, YOU PUSHED ME.
WHEN I COULD NOT MOVE,
YOU DID EVERYTHING FOR ME.

THE LAST THREE YEARS
HAS BEEN A ROLLERCOASTER.
YOU MADE ME SEE HOW STRONGER,
I MADE YOU FEEL.

MUM, YOU BELIEVED WITHIN ME
WHEN NO ONE ELSE DID.
THEY SAID I WAS IN DENIAL AND WON'T MAKE IT.
YOU KNEW I WOULD.

MUM, YOU CALL ME
THE STRONG ONE,
BUT I THINK I WAS SPARED.
I WAS IN A COMA AND REMEMBER NOTHING.

YET IT WAS YOU
WHO SAW THE NEEDLES, WIRES, AND MACHINES,
NOT TO MENTION ALL THOSE TUBES TO GO.
IT WAS YOU AND DAD, WHO STAYED.

NO ONE KNOWS HOW I SURVIVED
BUT I DO.
I SURVIVED BECAUSE OF YOU, MUM.
FOR YOU LOVE ME, AND I LOVE YOU.

TWO YEARS ON, MY HAIR IS BACK,
BLONDE AND CURLIER THAN EVER.
I CAN WALK ONCE AGAIN,
ALMOST RUMBA.

WHERE WOULD I BE
WITHOUT MY AMAZING MUM?
IN HEAVEN AND PARADISE,
THAT'S WHERE I WOULD BE.

MUM, YOU ARE MY REAL-LIFE HEROINE.
I WISH I COULD BE EVEN HALF THE WOMAN
YOU ARE,
EVEN A QUARTER WILL DO.

TO MY MUM,
THANK YOU FOR BEING YOU,
THANK YOU FOR BEING MY MUM.
TO MY MUM, I LOVE YOU!

DID YOU KNOW?

DID YOU KNOW THE LORD ABOVE
CREATED YOU
FOR ME TO LOVE?

HE PICKED YOU OUT
FROM ALL THE REST
AS IF HE KNEW
I WOULD LOVE YOU THE BEST.

IF I DIE BEFORE YOU DO,
I WILL WAIT AT THE GATES
OF HEAVEN FOR YOU.

I WILL HANG AROUND,
SO, YOU CAN FIND ME THERE.
THIS IS HOW I FEEL
WHEN I THINK OF YOU.

FRIENDS

THEY SAY,
THE WORLD IS FULL OF FRIENDS.
THEY COME IN DIFFERENT SHAPES AND SIZES.
SOME ARE OLD AND SOME ARE YOUNG,
OLD ONES AND NEW ONES.
SOME YOU HAVE GROWN UP WITH,
SOME YOU HAVE NEVER KNOWN.

THERE ARE THOSE
THAT WE KNOW ABOUT,
THOSE WE HAVE NEVER SEEN,
LIKE DEAR OLD SANTA CLAUS.
OUR LITTLE FRIEND THE TOOTH FAIRY,
THE GUARDIAN ANGELS,
WHO WATCH OVER US.

THEN YOU HAVE LITTLE BOYS
WHO DREAM OF BEING HEROES,
TO WIN THE HEARTS OF PRINCESSES.
WHO GAVE THEM NEVER-ENDING LOVE,
EVER SO DEARLY.
THE PRINCESS WHO DREAMS
OF HER TALL, BROWN EYED HERO,
WITH THE GOLDEN SILKY SKIN,
WITH A HEART OF GOLD.
WHO WILL LOVE AND PROTECT HER,
FOR HE IS HER HERO AND FRIEND.

THEY HAVE NEVER MET, BUT,
YET,
SUCH PERFECT FRIENDS,
IF ONLY,
THEY HAD MET!

IN HOSPITAL

SO, MY MUM JUST WENT HOME,
I AM HERE,
SITTING ON MY BED,
THINKING OF MY WONDERFUL FRIENDS.

VERY STILL,
VERY QUIET,
TICK TOCK
WENT THE CLOCK!

THANK GOODNESS FOR POETRY,
THANK GOD FOR FRIENDS,
FRIENDS WITH IMAGINATIONS,
POEMS, PHOTOS AND ART.

IF THE ILLNESS, WON'T KILL YOU,
IF THE PAIN, DOES NOT GET YOU,
WITHOUT MY FRIENDS,
BOREDOM SURELY WILL.

NURSES ARE OKAY,
ONLY I GOT DOC....HERE.

FOOD IS FINE, BUT
DASCHA'S FRUIT PICTURES ARE BETTER.

I AM HAPPY, RUDYARD'S POETRY MAKES IT NICER.
IT IS DULL, BUT YAZ AND ERROL ARE HERE.

NOT SURE ABOUT THIS PROF'
GOT REGELLE HOPE HERE FOR SECOND OPINION.

TRYING TO BE RELAXED,
MICHAEL IS HERE, MANTRA ALERT.
BAD MAGAZINES.... DANIEL, SAVES THE DAY.
MORE STOLEN APPLES ON THE WAY, LOVE TO READ.

LAST TIME I WAS IN HOSPITAL,
I HAD MY TEDDY BEAR, BUT IT WAS STOLEN.
NO, NOT ALONE, DIPSI IS HERE.
THERE GOES PATRCIA WITH HER NO
PLACE LIKE HOME RED SHOES!

PATRICIA AND EVA BOTH
SAYING.... 'TAP THE SHOES'
SAY 'NO PLACE LIKE HOME THREE TIMES,'
FOLLOW THE YELLOW LINE DOWN THE CORRRIDOR,
OOPS! DIDN'T WORK, STILL IN HOSPITAL.

BUT AT LEAST, EVEN THOUGH HERE ALONE,
MY FRIENDS WERE HERE IN SPIRIT,
MAKING ME LAUGH.
BOY, HAS TIME FLOWN FAST.
NOW IT IS HOME TIME!
GREAT!

CLOSE YOUR EYES!

CLOSE YOUR EYES
AND THINK OF ME.
REACH OUT AND HOLD MY HANDS,
HOLD THE GAZE.

WITH ME,
NOTHING HURTS.
WITH ME,
YOU FEEL LOVE.

WHAT DO YOU DRINK?
AH, PINA COLARDA.
WHERE DO YOU THINK?
OH, IN DORADO.

OH NO....
THE DOCTOR COMES,
THE NUSRE IS HERE,
BABY, CLOSE YOUR EYES.

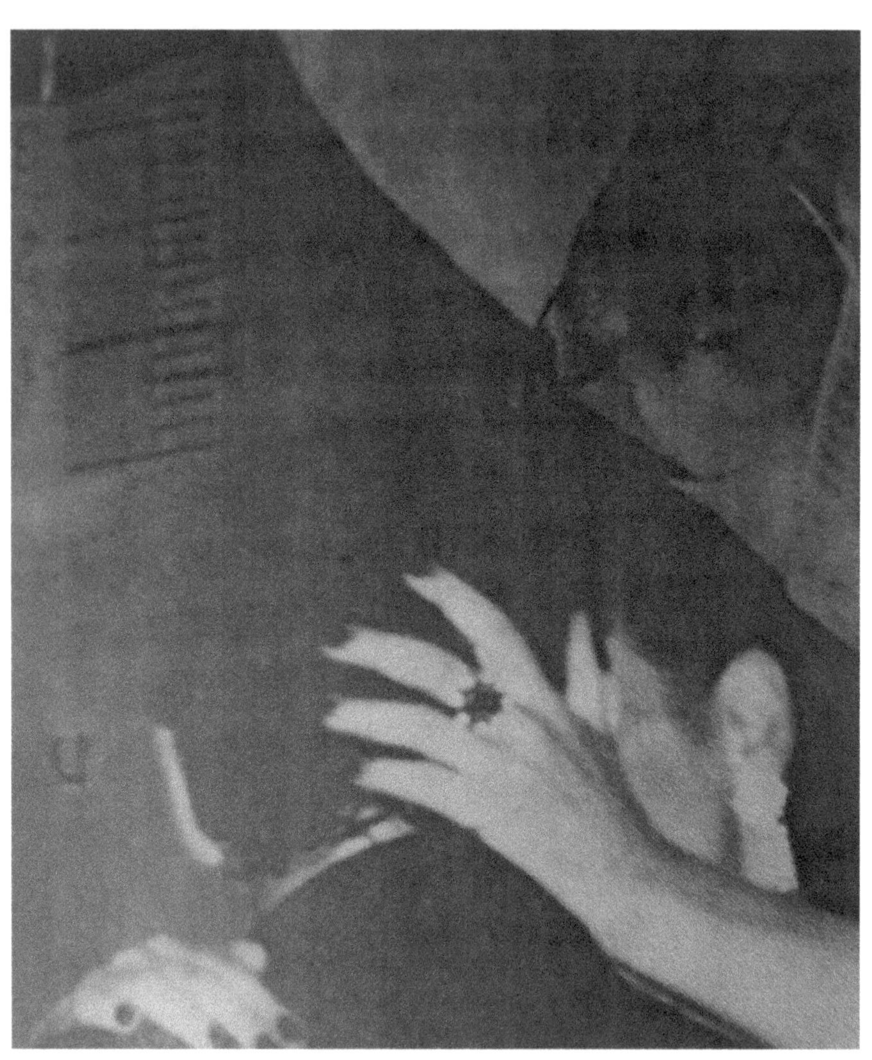

SMILE FOR ME,
SAY MY NAME,
CLOSE YOUR EYES,
FLY TO ME.

HERE COMES THE NEEDLE,
HERE COMES THE COOL,
BABY, COUNT 1,2, 3.
COME DANCE WITH ME.

THE RUMBA , THE SAMBA,
THE ZUMBA,
THE BOSSA NOVA,
THE TANGO.

THEY SAY, 'IT TAKES TWO TO TANGO,'
THEY SAY, 'ONE TO FLEMENCO,'
THEY SAY, 'THREE TO BE FAMILY,'
SO, BABY, LIVE FOR ME.

BABY, CLOSE YOUR EYES,
WAKE UP.
I AM HERE!

MEMORY OF A LITTLE ANGEL, EDWARD THURSTON

TO MY WONDERFUL LOVING MUMMY,
THANK YOU FOR LOVING ME, ADOPTING ME
WHEN NO ONE ELSE IN THE WORLD WANTED ME.

I MAY HAVE SHARED MY TINY PRECIOUS LIFE
FOR JUST A SHORT BEAUTIFUL WHILE,
BUT YOU GAVE ME THE BEST
THE OTHERS DREAM AN ENTIRE LIFE WISHING.

PLEASE DON'T CRY AND BLAME YOURSELVES,
REMEMBER ALL THE AWESOME TIMES,
COUNTING FINGERS AND TOES,
MUMMY SINGING AND DADDY PLAYING THE PIANO.

REMEMBER HOW HAPPY YOU WERE
BEFORE MY SHORT LIFE CAME TO UP HERE,
SMILE AND BE HAPPY,
FOR I WAS.

YOU BLESSED ME WITH THE MIRACLE
OF A HAPPY LOVING HOME,
SO, IN RETURN,
YOU ARE HAVING A MIRALCE OF A GIFT.

YOU DID NOT WANT MY PRECIOUS LIFE
TO LIVE ALONE, SO, YOU TOOK ME IN.
EVEN WITH MY CANCER,
YOU LOVED ME LIKE YOUR OWN.

I LOVE YOU SO MUCH, SO I'M SENDING YOU A FRIEND,
MY BROTHER, DON'T FEEL GUILTY
FOR HAVING YOUR OWN.
MUMMY, HE WILL BE LOVED AND SAFE.
FOR I KNOW, I TRULY WAS.

REMEMBER ME . . . . ANGEL, EDWARD THURSTON.

KNOW ...

I DON'T KNOW WHY?
WHAT TO THINK?
WHAT TO FEEL?
OR EVEN, WHAT TO SAY?

ALL I KNOW
IS WHEN I THINK OF YOU,
I FEEL HAPPY AND ALIVE.

YOU MAKE ME FEEL
LIKE SUMMER HOLIDAYS AND
STRAWBERRY ICE CREAM,
SWEET COCONUT.

WHEN I HEAR YOUR VOICE,
I FEEL LIKE, I AM IN PARADISE,
ORCHIDS, ROSES, AND LILLIES.

WHEN I SMELL YOUR COLOGNE,
I THINK KISSES AND CUDDLES
WITH CUDDLY TEDDY BEARS.
ALL ROLLED UP INTO ONE.

I DON'T KNOW WHY? COS,
I HAVE NOT MET YOU.
FOR YOU LIVE WITHIN MY DREAMS.

RUDYARD BONILLA

IF THERE EVER WAS A TIME,
I WANTED TO WISH A FRIEND,
A HAPPY BIRTHDAY,
IT WOULD BE RUYARD BONILLA.

A MAN, WHO IS A DEAR FRIEND.
WITH A MIND AS NICE AS HOT CHOCOLATE,
SWEET AS THE SUMMER BREEZE,
IT WOULD BE RUDYARD BONILLA.

A MAN WITH A HEART
AS WARM AS THE SUMMER SUN,
POEMS AS SWEET AS MANGOES,
IT WOULD BE RUDYARD BONILLA.

A MAN WITH A BEAUTIFUL WIFE,
BRIDGET, ALSO, A DARLING FRIEND.
ANGLES BLESS HIS SOUL, HIS BELOVED SONS,
IT WOULD BE RUDYARD BONILLA.

A MAN I WISH THE WARMEST
WISHES AND DREAMS, HAPPY DAYS AND
LIVES, IT WOULD BE RUDYARD BONILLA.

A MAN I WISH *HAPPY BIRTHDAY!*
IS YOU, MY FRIEND RUDYARD BONILLA.

SOMEONE TOLD ME!

SOMEONE SAID BEING AN ADULT WAS EASY,
SOMEONE SAID BE A BABY WAS EASY,
NO ONE SAID TWO TO EIGHTY WAS EASY.

SOMEONE SAID SCHOOL IS THE
BEST DAYS OF YOUR LIFE,
SOMEONE SAID BEING A WIFE WAS BEST FOR YOU,
NO ONE SAID BEING A REAL FRIEND WAS HARD.

SOMEONE SAID BEING A MOTHER
WILL BE THE MAKING OF YOU,
SOMONE SAID LIFE MAKES YOU STRONGER,
NO ONE SAID IT IS PAINFUL.

SOMEONE SAID BIG GIRLS DON'T CRY,
SOMONE SAID BIG BOYS DON'T FEEL PAIN,
NO ONE TOLD ME THAT.

SOMEONE TOLD ME LIFE HAS NO GUARANTEES,
SOMEONE TOLD ME LIFE HAS NO WARRANTEES,
NO ONE SAID 'NO' TO A PROMISE.

SOMEONE SAID LIFE WON'T BE CRUEL,
SOMEONE SAID YOU WILL NEVER BE ALONE,
KNOWING I AM ALL ALONE.

SOMEONE SAID YOU LIVE OLD,
SOMEONE SAID YOU WILL SUCCEED,
NO ONE TOLD ME THAT.

SOMEONE TOLD ME LIFE WAS FOREVER POSITIVE,
SOMEONE TOLD ME YOU ALWAYS MAKE IT,
NO ONE TOLD ME THAT.

SOMEONE SAID YOU ALWAYS BE HEALTHY,
SOMEONE SAID THEY ALWAYS BE FAMILY,
NO ONE TOLD ME THAT.

SOMEONE SAID THERE ARE COOKBOOKS,
SOMEONE SAID THERE ARE BOOKS,
NO ONE TOLD ME OF A LIFE BOOK!

SOMEONE IS TELLING YOU.
I DON'T KNOW.
SO DON'T BLAME ME; IF I NEVER GET IT,
I NEVER HAD IT; TO GIVE IT.

I AM

I AM HAPPY EVERYIME THE SUN RISES,
I AM HAPPY EVERYTIME THE STARS COME OUT,
I AM WHEN I SEE THE BEAUTIFUL MOON,
I AM HAPPY WHEN I SEE THE BLUE OR GREY SKIES.

I AM HAPPY WHEN A NEWBORN BABY ARRIVES,
I AM HAPPY WHEN ANOTHER ANIMAL IS BORN,
I AM HAPPY WHEN TREES AND CROPS ARE GROWN,
I AM HAPPY AT THE CITY OR THE BEACH.

I AM HAPPY WHEN SOMEONE SINGS,
I AM HAPPY SOMEONE READS AND WRITES,
I AM HAPPY WHEN SOMEONE PASSES AN EXAM,
I AM HAPPY WHEN SOMEONE JUST DID THEIR EXAMS.

I AM HAPPY WHEN PEOPLE SMILE AND LAUGH,
I AM HAPPY WHEN SOMEONE GETS MARRIED,
I AM HAPPY WHEN SOMEONE SHARES,
I AM HAPPY WHEN THERE IS HUMANITY.

I AM SAD WHEN SOMEONE CRIES,
I AM SAD WHEN SOMEONE HURTS,

I AM SAD WHEN THERE IS LONELINESS,
I AM SAD WHEN THERE IS WAR.

I AM SAD WHEN PEOPLE ARE MEAN,
I AM SAD WHEN THERE IS VIOLENCE IN THE WORLD,

I AM SAD WHEN PEOPLE FIND
PLEASURE OF BOXING FIGHTS,
I AM SAD WHEN PEOPLE FIND
PLEASURE IN ARGUMENTS.

I AM ANGRY WHEN A PERSON ABUSES OTHERS,
I AM ANGRY WHEN PEOPLE ACT
CRIMINAL FOR NO REASON,
I AM ANGRY THAT SOME PEOPLE HAVE NOTHING,
I AM ANGRY THAT SOME CHILDREN ARE NOT LOVED.

WHAT I LOVE THE MOST,
IS THE LOVE . . . .
THAT UNITES AND COMBINES THE WORLD . . . .
IF YOU LOOK CLOSE ENOUGH, YOU WILL SEE.

LOVE IS SOMETHING SO POWERFUL
IF DONE RIGHT.
YOU CAN FEEL IT, SEE IT, HEAR IT.
LOVE IS SADNESS, PAIN, SORROW, JOY,
WARMTH AND HARMONY.

DIVERSE COMPASSION
LOVE THE WORLD, AND THE WORLD WILL LOVE YOU!
THIS IS ME.... DON'T KNOW ABOUT YOU?
LOVE FOR THE WORLD!

NO, I'M DREAMING

BLUE SKY,
WHITE FLUFFY CLOUDS,
GOLDEN YELLOW SUN,
GREEN GRASS,
RED ROSES.

TERRACOTTA POTS,
GREEN GRAPES,
BIG BICEPS,
AH HA, A SIX-PACK.

BROWN EYES,
BROWN HAIR,
GOLDEN BROWN SKIN,
BRILLIANT WHITE TEETH.

MANGO SORBET,
CHOCOLATE CAKE,
PINA COLARDA,
KISS ON THE LIPS.

ROSIE CHEEKS,
GOLDEN LOCKS,
GREEN EYES,
MILKY SKIN

EYE TO EYE,
HAND IN HAND,
RICE AND PEAS, HMMM,
THE SALSA.

MUST BE IN LOVE?
MUST BE I'M DRUNK.
MUST BE DAFT.
NO, I'M DREAMING.

(TRIBUTE TO THE LIFE OF WONDERFUL
BELOVED UNCLE GLENN)

FOREVER MY UNCLE

IT WAS A SHOCK TO MY SYSYTEM
TO DISCOVER YOU PASSED AWAY
AS I LAY IN HOSPITAL CRITICAL.
ONE DAY I COME OUT OF A COMA,
AND YOU'RE ON THE TELEPHONE,
THE NEXT DAY . . . . YOU HAVE PASSED AWAY.

IT IS ALMOST THREE YEARS SINCE YOU WENT AWAY,
I AM SELFISHLY SAD....
FOR, I CAN'T HUG YOU LIKE BEFORE.
HOWEVER, IN MY HEART, I AM HAPPY,
FOR YOU ARE HAPPY AND PAIN FREE.

WHENEVER MY MIND WAS TROUBLED,
UNCLE, YOU WERE THERE FOR ME.
WHENEVER I WAS SAD,
YOU ALWAYS HUGGED ME.

WHENEVER I WAS UPSET,
YOU MADE ME LAUGH.
WHEN I WAS ILL OR HURT,
NO MATTER WHAT, YOU DROVE TO THE HOSPITAL.

WHEN OTHERS PUT ME DOWN,
YOU MADE ME BELIEVE WITHIN MYSELF,
YOU SAW MY TALENTED DREAMS,
MADE ME FIGHT PASSIVELY FOR THEM.

SOMETIMES MY EDUCATION AND EXAMS,
WERE BAD AND SEEMED BORING.
BUT YOU PUSHED ME TO GO ON,
WHEN OTHERS TRIED TO PUSH ME INTO THINGS.

YOU REMINDED ME, WHAT A REAL LADY IS,
FOR THAT, I THANK YOU.

MY BELOVED UNCLE....
NO MATTER WHAT....
I KNOW YOU'RE ALWAYS HERE....
IN SOME WAY OR THE OTHER....
FOR A SOUL IS ENERGY AND ENERGY CANNOT DIE....
IT MERELY TRANSFORMS FROM ONE
FORMAT TO ANOTHER.

UNCLE, PEOPLE TELL ME,
I AM A REAL LADY, AND THEY DON'T
MAKE THEM ANYMORE.
MY NANA AND MUM HAVE TAUGHT ME WELL.
STILL, YOU TAUGHT ME THOSE QUALITIES AS WELL.
I WANT YOU TO KNOW....
I ALWAYS LOVE YOU .... STILL DO...AND FOREVER WILL.

WHEN I NEED YOU....
I JUST CALL AND YOU COME....
SOME MAY SAY IT'S ME DREAMING ON OLD TIMES.

ONLY, I DON'T CARE....
FOR MEMORIES ARE THE BEST EVER.

YOU ALWAYS CALLED ME YOUR DOWNEY ROSE,
SO ON MY BIRTHDAY, I PLANTED
A BEAUTIFUL ROSEBUSH,
JUST FOR YOU.... I CALL IT, UNCLE'S ROSES.

THANK YOU FOR BEING MY UNCLE,
THANK YOU FOR BEING MY BEST FRIEND,
THANK YOU FOR BEING MY GUARDIAN ANGEL,
MOST OF ALL, THANKS FOR BEING SIMPLY YOU.

I LOVE YOU.... UNCLE!

BABY CHRISTMAS

IT WAS A COLD; LONELY, AND BITTTER NIGHT,
BEEN LIVING ROUGH IN A STORM SHELTER,
JUST OF CENTRAL PARK.

NEVER USED TO,
WE HAD A BEAUTIFUL HOME BEFORE.
WE, I MEAN MUM AND DAD,
SISTER MASSIE, AND BROTHER TIM,
WITH OUR DOG CUDDLES.

ONLY IN FEBRUARY,
DAD LOST HIS JOB AT THE FIRM,
MUM WAS HAVING A PART TIME,
BETWEEN SCHOOL HOURS,
DAD CALLED IT RECESSION,
MUM CALL IT 'NIGHTMARE ON PLAZA STREET'.

IN APRIL, MUM LOST HER JOB AS WELL,
IT'S NO ONE'S FAULT – JUST LIFE.
SAID THE BOSS: GLOBAL CREDIT CRUNCH,
EVERYONE HAS TO MAKE BUDGET CUTS.

IN MAY, THEY TOOK THE HOUSE,
WE HAD TO MOVE TO AN APARTMENT,
WE HAD TO CHANGE SCHOOLS,
LIVE IN A CREEPY AREA.

I AM EIGHT, MASSIE IS TWELVE
AND TIMMY IS FOURTEEN.
MUM FOUND OUT SHE WAS PREGNANT.
DAD FOUND A CASUAL JOB, FOUR HOURS A DAY.
PAID THE RENT AND SOME FOOD AT LEAST.

I DON'T HAVE THAT MANY FRIENDS,
BECAUSE MY DAD IS AMERICAN
AND MY MUM, IS LATINA.
IT CAN BE HARD, BUT LOVE GIVES STRENGTH,
SO, MY MUM AND DAD SAY: 'TRUE LOVE IS FROM GOD'.

NO MATTER WHAT LIFE THROWS YOU,
NEVER CURSE AND ALWAYS WATCH YOUR TONGUE.
I REMEMBER GRANDMOTHER SAYING,
BEFORE THE CANCER GOT HER,
FOR SHE SMOKED MORE THAN A CHIMNEY.

COME SEPTEMBER,
EVERYONE WAS UNEMPLOYED,
THE ONLY JOBS WERE FOR SERVICE
PEOPLE AND POLICE,
DAD WAS AN ACCOUNTANT,
AND MUM, A DRAMA TEACHER.
BUT IT ALL FORECLOSED.

BY OCTOBER, THE BALIFFS CAME,
THE APARTMENT WAS GONE AND MY TOYS,
EVERYTHING WAS GONE.
MUM'S KEYS WOULD NOT WORK ANYMORE.
ALL WE HAD WAS $300.00 FROM THE ATM.

FOR A FEW WEEKS, WE STAYED ON SOFAS,
WITH FRIENDS OF MUM'S AND DAD'S.
MUM AND ME. . . . HERE,
DAD AND TIMMY. . . . THERE,
MASSIE AT THER SCHOOL FRIENDS.

IT DID'T LAST LONG.
WE WERE IN THE WAY,
FRIENDS BEGAN TO FIGHT,
WE HAD TO LEAVE.

MUM SOLD THREE BAGS OG
CLOTHES, TO PAY FOR FOOD.
TILL WE HAD ONE BACKPACK EACH.
A LITTLE ONE FOR THE COMING BABY.

IT WAS NOVEMBER, NOW SLEEPING IN PARKS,
TIMMY AND DAD HAVE BEEN ARRESTED.
PINCHING FRUIT TO FEED US.
MUM KEEPS MASSIE CLOSE,
FOR BOYS AND MEN KEEP LOOKING.

I THINK PEOPLE ARE BLIND, FOR THEY WALK BY.
NO ONE CARES; WE GO PLACE TO PLACE,
LIKE MARY AND JOSPEH,
BUT EVERY HOTEL, HOSTEL AND INN, ARE FULL.

IT IS FREEZING, MY SKIN ALL DRY AND ROUGH.
MY HAIR NOT GREAT, BUT IT'S COMBED.
IT RAINED LAST NIGHT AND WE GOT WET,
MUM NOT SO GOOD, SHE LOOKS PALE,

CAN'T USE THE STORM SHELTER WITH THE RAIN,
SO, DAD BROUGHT US TO AN ABANDONED GARAGE.
GOT TO BE CAREFUL,
WITH THE GANGS AND BAD ONES.
DAD HAS A COUGH.

DAD CALLS THIS ADVENTURE AND EXPLORATION,
LIKE HUCKLEBERRY FINN, IT'S SURVIVAL.
MAKES US LAUGH, LIKE JIM CAREY,
GOOFING AROUND.

IT'S WET; COLD, RAINING, AND NOW SNOWING.
SHOP WINDOWS OF FESTIVE GOODS,
SMELL OF TURKEY IN THE AIR,
BEER, AS WELL AS THE REST.

PEOPLE IN NEW YORK DRESSED TO THE NINES,
SHOPPING STILL IN BLOOMINGDALE, MUM USED TOO.
PRETTY GIRLS WITH PRETTY CLOTHES.
ME IN RAGS, LIKE CINDERELLA,
ONLY WITH MORE HOLES.

MUM'S STOMACHACHE IS GETTING WORSE,
SHE CAN BARELY STAND,
NO MONEY, FULL STOP.
NO BED FOR THE BABY, SOON IT WILL BE A BOX.

IT IS THE EVE OF NOEL NOW.
7.00 P.M OF 24 DECEMBER AND MUM CRIES,
'GET YOUR DAD, IT'S TIME, IT'S TIME. . . . '
IT'S COMING NOW,
TIMMY GOES AND FETCHES HIM.

DAD CARRIES HER TOWARDS THE
BACK OF THE GARAGE.
LIGHTS A BIGGER FIRE IN AN OIL DRUM,
THE BABY COMES AND IT'S A GIRL.
DAD NAMED TIMMY, TIMMY NAMED MASSIE,
MASSIE NAMED ME . . . . SO NOW MY TURN.

SHE WAS WHITE, NOT LIKE MASSIE, ALL GOLDEN.
HER EYES WERE GREEN LIKE DAD'S.
SHE HAD A SMILE. . . . SHE LOOKS AT ME.
I NAME HER CHRISTMAS!

MUM GETS THE SHAKES, SHE'S NOT MOVING.
DAD SCREAMS FOR SOMEONE TO COME,
NO ONE COMES.
TIMMY GOES WITH DAD TO FIND HELP.
A MAN HEARS . . . . A KIND MAN WITH A SMILE,
HAPPY EYES, LIKE GRANDMOTHER'S. . . .

HE HAS A CAR AND WITH FRIENDS.
THEY HAVE CELL PHONES AND THEY'RE NICE.
HIS NAME IS SEAN, SEAN WRENCH
(HA, HA, 007) SEAN SAYS HE CAN HELP
WITH A MEAL AND SOMEWHERE TO REST.

HE KNOWS PEOPLE WHO ARE HUMANITARIANS.
THEY HELP HOMELESS FAMILIES AND PEOPLE.
HE DOES WHAT HE CAN AND CHRISTMAS LIKES HIM.
HE SAYS, IT'S NOT MUCH, BUT IT'S SOMETHING.

I GUESS THERE IS HOPE, AFTER ALL.

EVER HAD ONE OF THOSE NIGHT

EVER HAD ONE OF THOSE NIGHTS?
WHEN ALL YOU DID WAS TOSSED AND TURNED,
YOU'RE IN YOUR BED FOR THE BEST OF THREE HOURS.
THE LIGHT IS OFF AND A HINT OF MOON,
YET YOU CANNOT SIMPLY SLEEP?

FIRST YOU TRIED A WARM BATH.
THEN YOU TRIED HOT CHOCOLATE.
THEN YOU TRIED COUNTING SHEEP.
THEN YOU TRIED PRAYERS, NOW YOUR MEDITATION.

NO, STILL YOU CANNOT SLEEP,
WHAT DID I DO TODAY?
WHAT DID I NOT DO?
HAVE I FORGOTTEN SOMETHING?
WELL, IT'S NOT THE KIDS, FOR THEY'RE IN BED.

I PLAY WITH MY HANDS. IT'S MY WEDDING RING.
I TURNED TO MY RIGHT SIDE, BUT YOU'RE NOT THERE.
I LOOK FOR YOUR MOBILE, BUT IT'S NOT THERE,
I LOOK FOR MINE, IT'S DOWNSTAIRS. WHERE ARE YOU?

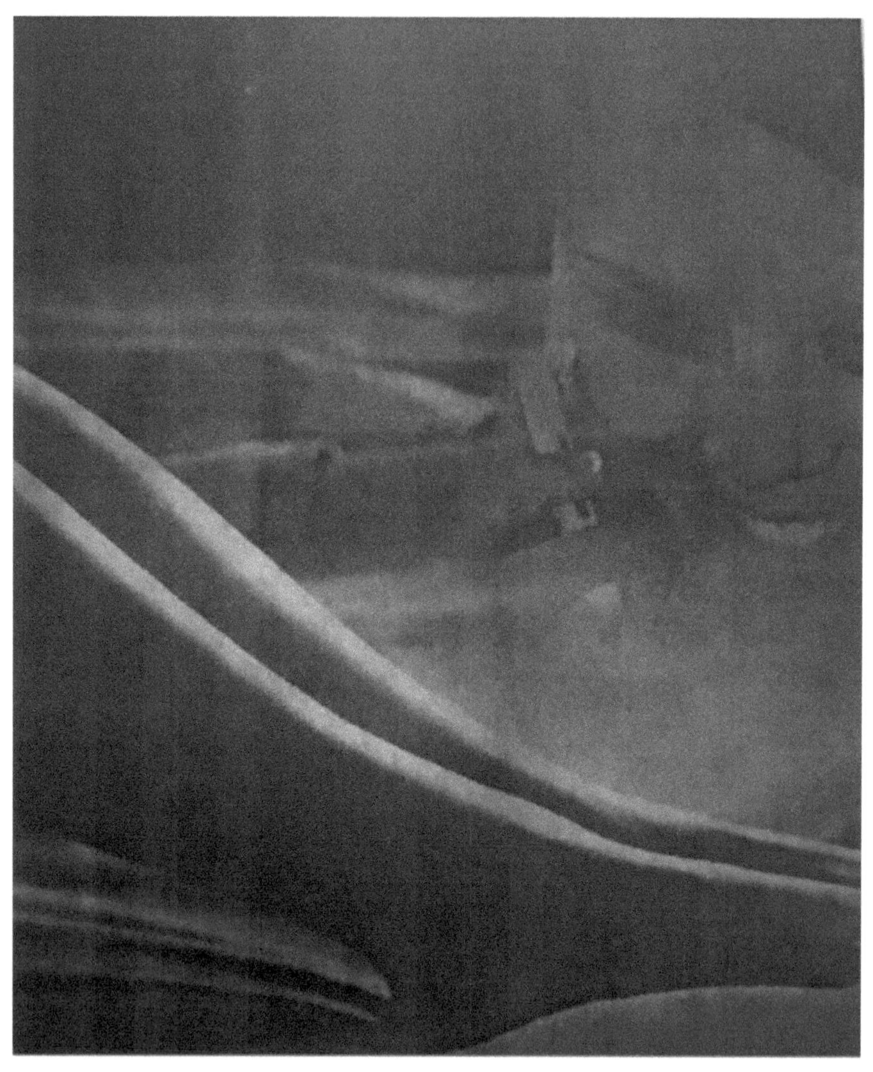

DOWN THE STAIRS IN THE DARK,
FETCH MY PHONE, IT'S GOT A TEXT.
IT'S FROM YOU, IN YOUR HOTEL BED,
ON TOUR, MISSING ME AND THE KIDS.
I KNOW WHY I CANNOT SLEEP?

FOR I FORGOT TO PHONE,
SAY 'GOODNIGHT AND GOD BLESS',
THE KIDS ARE COOL,
OH YES, I MISS YOU TOO!

EVER HAD ONE OF THOSE NIGHTS?

NO?

NOR ME!

NOT LIKE ME?

DON'T KNOW WHAT I DO?
I CAN THINK, CAN'T SLEEP,
CAN'T EAT,
NOT LIKE ME?

I CAN'T DREAM, I CAN'T WRITE,
I CAN'T SING, CAN'T PLAY THE PIANO,
NOT LIKE ME?

MY THROAT IS TIGHT, MY LEGS SHAKE,
MY HANDS SWEATY, MY FINGERS TWIDDLE,
NOT LIKE ME?

I CAN'T TELEPHONE, I CAN'T EMAIL,
I CAN'T FAX, I CAN'T TEXT,
NOT LIKE ME?

I CAN'T SPEAK, I CAN'T HEAR,
I CAN'T SEE. WHY ME?
WHAT IS WRONG WITH ME?

I SEE YOU; IT TICKLES ME, MAKES ME GIGGLE,
LIKE A LITTLE GIRL.
I THINK I LIKE YOU!

NOTHING LIKE THE COUNTRYSIDE!

THERE IS NOTHING LIKE THE COUNTRYSIDE,
COWS AND PIGS IN THE PLAYING FIELDS.
NOTHING LIKE WASHING CLOTHES,
WHEN FARMER JON IS MAKING CHEESE.

NOTHING LIKE THE COUNTRYSIDE,
GREEN, GREEN GRASS.
FRESH FLOWERS,
MAKING THE SNEEZE ALL DAY.

NOTHING LIKE THE COUNTRYSIDE,
HAVING A SUNDAY DRIVE,
FARMER JON ON A TRACTOR AT 5 MPH,
PETROL STATION SHUT AGAIN, IT'S ONY 6. OO P.M.

NOTHING LIKE THE COUTRYSIDE,
HAYS, WHEAT, AND HOBS.
FINE YOUNG MEN WITH PHONE NUMBERS,
BUT THEY GOT NO RECEPTION!

NOTHING LIKE THE COUNTRYSIDE!

DREAMING OF SINGING MY SONG

LONG BORING DAY, HE HAD.
STUCK IN A COACH,
GOING, OH NO, NOWHERE,
AT THIS BLOOMING RATE?

INCH BY INCH,
CREEK BY CREEK.
WENT THE SLOW DRIVE,
TO WHEREVER?

BEEN UP EARLY,
SHE THOUGHT.
NOT LIKE ME,
MUST BE ILL.

OH JUST, GREAT.
JUST MY MUM AND ME.
IT IS OKAY, BUT?
SCREAMING SCHOOL KIDS.

WITH THREE HOURS THERE,
TO WHO KNOWS WHERE?
FOR ONE HOUR THERE,
THEN FIVE HOURS FROM THERE.

STARTING HEAVY DOWNCAST,
IT'S GETTING COLD,
IT'S RAINING, IT'S FREEZING,
I'M HUNGRY.

OH WELL, JUST ANOTHER DAY.
ON THE ROAD COULD BE WORSE.
COULD BE A TRANSIT VAN.
NOT EVERYONE HAS A POSH RV,
NOT EVERYONE HAS A PA,
NOT EVERYONE IS A VIP,
NO, AFRAID, IT'S JUST ME.

SITTING HERE,
THINKING BACK.
I WAS YOUNG, WITH A DREAM,
GOT KIDS, WHAT'S HAPPENED?

GIVE IT UP? NEVER!
STILL DREAMING,
STILL MAKING,
STILL SINGING.

GROUPIES, ME? NEVER!
DID HAVE HER INDOORS,
ALL RIGHT FOR A WHILE,
BUT SHE DIDN'T WANT OUTDOORS.

THE WHEELS GROAN,
I REMEMBER HER MOAN,
I REMEMBER HER TONE,
MY THROAT WAS DRY AS A BONE.

THE ONLY THING STILL THE SAME.
IS THE LONG ROAD,
DRINKING BOTTLED WATER,
DREAMING OF SINGING MY SONG.

WHAT CAN £5.00 DO?

EVERY DAY FROM MONDAY TO FRIDAY,
I AM GIVEN £5.00 FOR LUNCH,
MOST OF THE TIME, I USE £3.30.
KEEP THE CHANGE. WHICH LEAVES ME WITH £8.50.

BY FRIDAY, THAT BECOMES £8.00,
SO THEREFORE, COME SATURDAY,
I CAN USE ANOTHER £3.30 FOR SALSA.
THAT LEAVES ME £4.70 TO BLOW ON SWEETS!

SO, I GOT THINKING,
WHAT WAS THAT £3.30 BEING SPENT ON?
EXTRA VALUE MEALS THAT IS WHAT?
DO I REALLY NEED ALL THAT?
NO, NOT REALLY.

I CAN JUST AS WELL GET ENERGY FROM
£1.99 MEALS, WHICH CONTAINS:
1 X DRINK, SMALL FRIES, SMALL BURGER
OR 1 X DRINK, SMALL PASTA SALAD WITH FRUIT.

SO, IF I SPENT £1.99 A DAY FOR SIX DAYS,
I AM MERELY SPENDING £11.94,
SO, OUT OF MY £25.00, I HAVE CHANGE OF £13.06.
AFTER SALSA ON SATURDAYS, I CAN USE £2.00.

WHICH THEN LEAVES WITH £11.06 ON SWEETS.
BUT DO I NEED SO MUCH SUGAR?
WELL, NO ACTUALLY.

I RATHER HAVE FRUIT; COME TO
THINK OF IT, IT'S CHEAPER.

SO, £11.06 IS WHAT I HAVE; STRAWBERRIES
AND PEARS COME TO £1.50,
A MANGO FOR GRAN COMES TO £1.60; MUM
LOVES HER GRAPES AT £1.99. SO, ALL TOGETHER
I SPENT £5.09, NOW I TREAT MYSELF AND
FAMILY, WHAT DO I DO WITH £5.09, NOW?

IF I AM IN ENGLAND, I CAN HELP
HOMELESS CHILDREN GET FED.
A HAPPY MEAL FOR KIDS AT
MCDONALD'S IT'S £1.99 EACH,
SO, I CAN EITHER FEED
TWO KIDS OR A PARENTS AND A CHILD,
I SHOULD GIVE IT TO CENTRE POINT!
LEAVING £1.19 FOR ME!

IF I WAS IN NEW YORK, I COULD
DO EXACTLY THE SAME,
ONLY, GIVE IT TO 'FORSAKEN YOUTH
GENERATION PROJECT!'
SO, THIS WEEK, I FED MYSELF AND
TREATED MY LOVED ONES.

WOW.... £5.00 CAN FEED FIVE PEOPLE!

SO, I HELPED SAVE PEOPLE'S LIVES,
LEARNT TO MANAGE MONEY,
LEARNT TO EAT PROPERLY, DID MY SALSA,
AND MADE A POSITIVE DIFFERENCE!
WHAT DID YOU DO, WITH YOUR £5.00?

FOR THE LOVE
OF APRODITE

OH, FOR THE LOVE OF APHRODITE,
HOW MY HEART CRIES?
BEEN THREE THOUSAND YEARS,
SINCE I WAS LAST HERE.

MY; MY, HAS TIME CHANGED.
BOYS AND MEN ARE NO LONGER THE SAME.
WAS A TIME WHEN ALL BUT FIFTEEN A
BOY WAS CONSIDERED A MAN.

LITTLE DID I KNOW.
I, THE MIGHTY APHRODITE,
THAT NOW IT TAKES TWICE AS LONG,
FOR IT IS THIRTY,
FOR A BOY TO BECOME A MAN.

BUT YET, IT IS STILL ME,
THAT LIVES WITHIN THEIR OATS.
TRUE, THEY DO MORE HOUSEWORK.
STILL IT IS ME, THEY LOVE.

ALL WITHIN THREE THOUSAND YEARS,
MUCH AS CHANGED IN THE WAYS,
OF MAN AND HIS KIND,
BUT THE LUST OF SHALLOWNESS!

THEY STILL LOVE AND YEARN FOR MY PERFECTIONS,
THE DESIREABLE AND TASTEFUL APHRODITE.
MY GREEN EYES, MILKY SKIN.
MY GOLDEN LONG GODDESS CURLY HAIR.

THE PERFECT SIZE 12, WITH THE ADDED
NATURAL CURVES TO LOVE,
TO LUST, TO CRAVE, TO YEARN,
FOR IT IS THE NAME OF APHRODITE THEY CRY,
ON THE HIGH SEAS, ON THE SHORES,
AND UPON THE NIGHTLY FEVER.

OH, HOW I STILL MAKE THEM FEVERISH,
RESTLESS NIGHTS, AND FUZZY BELLIES,
MOANING AND GROANING LIKE WOLVES
IN THE STILL OF THE NIGHT.

IT IS I, APHRODITE,
THAT MAKES YOU SMILE,
THAT MAKES YOU RUB YOUR ABS,
THE SMELL OF PERFUME, TOUCH OF MY SKIN.

THE THOUGHT OF ME INSIDE YOUR MIND,
IN YOUR HEARTS, AND ON YOUR SOUL.
MAKES YOU SWEAT AND LICK YOUR LIPS.
THE TOUCH OF MY HANDS MAKES YOU ALIVE.

WHERE THERE ARE ADVENTURES,
WHEREVER THERE ARE JOURNEYS,
ALL TRADERS, SAILORS, MERCHANTS
AND ENTERTAINERS,
FEEL NOT ALONE.

FOR I, APHRODITE, WALK AMOUNG YOU.

STAND ON THE SHORE AND STRUM ME A SONG,
I SHALL COME BY, SWEET ONE.
I HEAR THE SOUNDS OF YOUR LONELY CHEST DRUM,
FEAR NOT, I AM YOURS, YOUR APHRODITE!

AS HE SINGS AND STRUMS AWAY,
ALAS FOR THE LOVE OF APHRODITE!

IT WAS A FROSTY BITING NIGHT

IT WAS A FROSTY BITING NIGHT,
ALL AROUND WAS NO ONE TO BE FOUND.
FOR EVERY RAT AND SQUIRREL,
WAS EACH IN IT'S HOLE.

EVERY DOG AND CAT,
ASLEEP INDOORS BY THE CRACKLING FIRE.
OLD FARMER DORSET WITH WHISKY IN HAND,
MRS DORSET WITH HER BOURNEMOUTH BROTH.

EVERY CHILD FAST ASLEEP,
SNUG IN A WARM BED,
A CUDDLY TEDDY BEAR,
A MICROWAVEABLE BEAN BEAR!

ACROSS THE FIELD,
WAS A LONE FELLOW.
COLD, FREEZING AND IN PAIN.
IT WAS DEAR STEVE SHIVERING.

POOR STEVE WAS SO COLD,
WITH EXHAUSTION, HE FELL
ASLEEP, WARM SENSATIONS,
ALONG HIS CHEST.

AS IF HE WAS SUNBATHING,
AWAY IN SUNNY MIAMI.
A HINT OF CHANEL No.5,
A TASTE OF BICARDI AND COLA.

HE KNOWS AT ONCE, HE WAS BEING CARED FOR,
BY HIS LITTLE FRIEND TICKERBELL.
WHO LOVED DISNEY
AND GREW UP TO BE JUST FIVE FEET TALL.

IT WAS HER KISSES,
IT WAS HER HUGS,
IT WAS HER HAIR,
IT WAS HER!

A WALK IN THE PARK

AS SHE WENT ON HER WAY HOME,
AFTER A BUSY DAY AT THE OFFICE.
SHE CHOSE TO TAKE A SLOW WALK,
RIGHT THROUGH CENTRAL PARK.

IT WAS SEPTEMBER, AND THE LEAVES
WERE OF MANY COLOURS.
SOME WERE GREEN, ORANGE, RED,
GOLDEN AND BROWN.
IT HAD BEEN RAINING FOR MOST OF THE DAY.
AS THE EVENING APPROACHED,
THE EVENING WARMTH HAD ARRIVED.

THE SUN WAS SETTING, GIVING
THE SKY A PINKISH TONE.
THE RAIN WAS NOW VAPOUR AND THE MIST CAME.
AS SHE WALKED, SHE REMEMBERED HER LOVER,
OUT AT SEA.

SHE FELT LONELY, BUT NEVER ALONE,
FOR HE WAS FOREVER IN HER MIND, HEART AND SOUL.
SHE STARTED TO GROW COLD WITH THE
BREEZE OF THE AMERICAN FALL.
SHE IMAGINED THE MIST AROUND HER LIKE HIS ARMS.

NANA

THERE IS NO ONE IN THIS WORLD
WHO COULD EVER BE POSSIBLY
COMPARED TO MY NANA.
FOR SHE SIMPLY IS THE GREATEST,
JUST SIMPLY UNIQUE.

I HAVE NEVER MET ANYONE,
QUITE RATHER LIKE NANA, BEFORE OR SINCE.
A WARM LOVING WOMAN WITH A
DRY SENSE OF HUMOUR.
ONLY SHE AND ONE MORE COULD MAKE ME LAUGH.

MY NANA IS NOT LIKE EVERYONE
ELSE'S GRANDMOTHER.
NO, SHE IS SO DIVERSE AND YOUNG SPIRITED.
YOU WOULD NEVER TELL SHE WAS
MERELY EIGHTY SOMETHING.
PRETTY YOUNG ACTUALLY; IN
CHINA, THEY ARE LIKE 101.

SHE HAS ALWAYS BEEN THERE, COME RAIN OR SHINE,
AS LONG AS IT WAS GOOD FOR YOU.
THERE WAS NEVER ANYTHING SHE
WOULD NOT DO FOR YOU,
IF SHE COULD, SHE WOULD.

MY NANA IS A MODERN LADY WITH
TRADITIONAL VALUES.
NOTHING WRONG WITH THAT,
A RATHER REFINED BALANCE.
OF TRADITIONAL MORALS AND THE
WAY OF TODAY'S WORLD.
JUST HOW A LADY SHOULD ALWAYS BE.

I REALLY LOVE MY NANA
FOR SHE GAVE ME MY MUM,
WHO IN TURN,
GAVE ME,
WELL,
ME.

DIVERSE LOVE

HAVE YOU EVER EVEN WONDERED WHAT LOVE IS?
I MEAN WHAT IT REALLY IS?
WOULD WE EVEN KNOW IF WE HAD IT?
WOULD WE KNOW WE LOST IT?
WHETHER OR NOT WE EVEN EVER HAD IT?

IS LOVE SIMPLE OR IS IT COMPLEX?
I AM NOT SURE; GUESS IT DEPENDS
ON THE TYPE OF LOVE.
I SEEM TO LOVE ALL THE TIME, I DO ACTUALLY,
NOW I COME TO THINK ABOUT IT.

I LOVE MY FAMILY, MY PARENTS AND MY NEPHEWS.
I LOVE MY FRIENDS AND PEOPLE
I HAVE WORKED WITH.
I LOVE MY PETS, OTHER ANIMALS IN THE WORLD,
I EVEN LOVE PEOPLE AROUND THE WORLD. . .

I LOVE THE SKIES, OCEANS AND LANDSCAPES.
I LOVE DOING THINGS, LIKE MY
HOBBIES AND INTERESTS.
SOMETIMES I KNOW I AM LOVED AND THAT I LOVE.
I EITHER FEEL HAPPY WITH JOY OR SAD WITH PAIN.
IT IS ALL PART OF LOVE.

YOU CAN NEVER PUT LOVE IN A NUTSHELL....
THAT WOULD BE IMPOSSIBLE,
FOR LOVE COMES IN DIFFERENT WAYS,
SO, THE WAY I SEE IT . . .
THE SOUL CONTAINS DIVERSE LOVE!

DIVERSE LOVE

2025 COLLECTION

FORWARD BY MR. JOHNNY DEPP

I thank Mr.Johnny Depp for taking time from his busy schedule to do the ' Forward' for the 2025 Poetry Collection. I appreciate it. ~ Sharon.

MUSIC AS LOVE

MUSIC IS MY PASSION,
POETRY IS MY PASSION,
IN THE 1990'S RADIO WAS AN AN ALL MAN'S INDUSTRY.
SURE, THERE WERE WOMEN.
BUT THEY WERE NOT ALLOWED TO DO THE SAME,
GET HIGHT POSITIONS AS THE MEN.

TRUE, JANICE LONG AND ANNIE NIGHTINGALE,
BECAME THE FIRST FEMALE
RADIO PRESENTERS IN THE 1970'S.
TOOK THEM TWO DECADES TOO GAIN REPESCT.
MY HERO AND MENTOR,
BEST FRIEND, BIG SISTER FIGURE IS NO
OTHER THAN DJ SARAH HB.

SHE IS MORE THAN A RADIO PRESENTER
THAT NEEDS A SOUND ENGINEER,
TO WORK IN A SEPARATE ROOM
PUSHING BUTTONS AND SLIDDING
CHANNELS.
NO, IN FACT, SARAH CAN DRIVE A CONSOLE....
SHE IS A SPECIALST DJ IN 'HOUSE'. AND
SHE SURE KNOWS HOW TO MIX.

SHE TAUGHT ME, HOW TO DRIVE A CONSOLE.
HOW TO FEEL WITH MY SPIRIT,
MY FEET AND MY HANDS,
USING THE VIBRATIONS OF MUSIC....

ANYONE CAN LISTEN TO HEAR....
TO HOME OR ZEN IN,
ON TO ONE INSTRUMENT, BLOCK OUT THE SOUNDS.
OF EVERYTHING ELSE, AROUND YOU!

BACK IN THE 1990'S MY FRIEND SARAH HB,
WAS AND STILL IS A FORERUNNER, A PIONEER....
SHE STOOD UP TO MEN,
"WHAT, A WOMAN, PRODUCES OR MIX A TRACK?"

I AM SO HONOURED TO OF WORKED WITH SARAH
BECOME HER FRIEND.
THE COMPASSION, THE HUMANITY AND PATIENCE,
SHE SHOWED AND SHARED,
SHE STILL DOES....

AN INTERNATIONAL CLUBBING DJ
WHO DOES RADIO TOO!
FEMALE PIONEER.

THAT'S DEDICATION, THAT IS PASSION AND, YES,
THAT IS A FORM OF LOVE TOO.
SARAH KEEP GOING....
MUSIC AS LOVE....

THE ROMANCE LOVE COMPLEX

THEY SAY WHEN A MAN TRULY LOVES A
WOMAN, SHE BECOMES HIS WEAKNESS,
AND,
WHEN A WOMAN TRULY LOVES A MAN,
HE BECOMES HER STRENGTH....
SO, WHEN THEY DON'T COMMUNICATE AND,
FALL OUT OF SYNCHRONICITY HE FEELS LOST,
WITHOUT HER,
HE BACKS OFF....
WHILE SHE FEELS LOST WITHOUT HIM,
SHE BUGS HIM IN ATTENTION SEEKING....
TROUBLE IS THE MORE SHE BUGS HIM,
THE MORE HE BACKS OFF....
TRICK IS, SHE MUST BACK OFF AND LET HIM MISS HER
ONLY THEN HE CHASES FORWARD AFTER HER....
SIT CALMLY, TALK IT OUT,
SO THE COMMUNICATIONS RESTORE,
UNITED WITH SYNCHRONICITY,
AND THAT'S THE JOURNEY AND ADVENTURE,
THE ROMANTIC LOVE COMPLEX.

THE GREATEST LOVE

GREATEST LOVE THERE IS
HAS NO EXPECTATIONS
IS HUMBLE
LIKE CHEESE ON TOAST.

DON'T BE JUDGEMENTAL
BUT BE A JUDGE TO TEACH
RESPONSIBILITY KNOWS
GOOD FROM BAD
RIGHT FROM WRONG.

WAS IT GOOD
JUST BECAUSE IT WAS RIGHT
WAS IT BAD

LIFE IS NEVER AS IT SEEMS.
LOVE SOMEONE AS THEY ARE
FORGIVE THE PAST
MOVE FORWARD.
SOMETIMES IF TOXIC PERSONALITY
THAT NEVER AGREE
MAYBE IT'S FOR THE BEST
TO SIMPLY AVOID CONTACT
IN THE NAME OF PEACE AND LOVE.
THE GREATEST LOVE
RAISES YOUR ENERGIES
GIVES YOU SELF ESTEEM
RAISES YOUR CONFIDENCE.

AND, EVEN IF SHY
DON'T SIT DOWN, STAND UP
HOLDS HANDS IN SUPPORT.

KNOW SOMEONE'S PAST
UNDERSTAND WHY
YOU MAY NOT APPROVE
KEEP THAT TO YOURSELF.

THEY CHANGED THEIR LIFE AROUND
YOU WERE NOT WITH THEM THEN.
FOR ALL YOU KNOW, IT'S LOVING THEM NOW
THAT HAS PUT THE GREATEST LOVE INTO THEM.

JUST HEAR THEM OUT, KNOW WHEN TO BE STILL
HAVE NO EXPECTATION
YOU WON'T GET UPSET OR LET DOWN
REMEMBER THE THOUGHT COUNTS.

SOME PEOPLE FIND LOVE AND HAPPINESS BY
MAKING POSITIVE CHANGES TO THEIR LIFE
CHANGE OF JOB
CHANGE OF FRIENDS.
SOME PEOPLE FIND LOVE, HAPPINESS
AND JOY IN THE FUTURE
WHEN LIFE BRINGS THE GREATEST LOVE
THEY NEVER HAD.

HAVE NO EXPECTATIONS
JUST SHINE THE GREATEST LOVE.
HOW ARE YOU?
HOW WAS YOUR DAY?
LIKE A CUP OF TEA?
SEE YOU WHEN I SEE YOU.

SOME PEOPLE RUB EACH OTHER UP THE WRONG WAY
THEY CLASH, ALWAYS DISAGREE, NARCISSISTIC.
JUST WALK AWAY, LET THEM BE,
TO ENJOY THEIR LIVES IN PEACE.
PEACE AND FREEDOM FOR YOU....

SOME PEOPLE WERE NEVER LOVED OR CARED
FOR AS A CHILD.
SO, DON'T BE ANGRY IF YOU ARE
BLESSED AND HONOURED
THEY TREAT YOU LIKE A LOVING MUM OR DAD.

NO ONE LOVED THEM
THEY ARE SURVIORS
SO, THE FACT THEY CHOOSE YOU
PROVES HOW SAFE THEY FEEL WITH YOU.

IT IS NOT ABOUT LUST
IT'S ABOUT HOW SAFE, I FEEL WITH YOU.
WHO CARES THEY OUT WITH FRIENDS
BE BLESSED THEY GIVE YOU TIME TO YOURSELF.

LOVE IS DIVERSE
NO ONE IS PERFECT
IT'S NOT ALWAYS EASY
NOT ALWAYS HAPPY.

BUT THE GREATEST LOVE IS LIKE YIN AND THE YANG
ENOUGH IN COMMON TO RELATE
ENOUGH IN OPPOSITES TO AID
WHEN ONE IS DOWN, THE OTHER HOLDS HANDS
RASIES THEM TO A HIGHER LEVEL.

THE GREATEST LOVE IS NOT ALWAYS BEING THERE
DAY IN, DAY OUT
KISSES AND HUGS.

THE GREATEST LOVE IS UNDERSTANDING
COMPASSIONATE AND COMMUNICATIVE
IN ONE WAY OR ANOTHER.

ACCEPT THE PAST, ACKNOWLEDGE TODAY
ALL IN ALL PATIENCE, ALL IN GOOD TIME,
WITH THE GREATEST LOVE THE FUTURE WILL
WRITE ITSELF.
COMPLICATED?
GOOD
LIFE IS.

THE GREATEST LOVE KNOWS THIS.

SERVANDO

DONDE LOS CIELOS SON ROSAS,
EL SOL SE PONE BAJO,
HACER LA CALOR LA TARDE.

WHERE THE SKY IS PINK
THE SUN SET LOW
THE WARMTH OF EVENING

SERVANDO BAILA Y CANTA,
TOCCANDO SU GUITARRA ACÚSTICA,
UN CABELLERO DE CORAZÓN.

SERVANDO DANCES AND SINGS
STRUMMING HIS ACOUSTIC GUITAR
A GENTLEMAN OF HEART

LA MÚSICA NO PAGA EL ALGUILER SOLA,
SERVANDO EL DOCTOR DEL ENTRETENIMENTO,
UNA VOZ DEL ALMA TRAE LÁGRIMAS A LOS OJOS.

MUSIC DOESN'Y PAY THE RENT ALONE
SERVANDO THE DOCTOR OF ENTERTAINMENT
A VOICE OF SOUL BRINGING TEARS TO THE EYES.

SELF LOVE

IT'S HARD
BUT YOU CAN
IT'S TOUGH
BUT YOU CAN.
YOU FEEL PAIN
BUT YOU CAN
YOU FEEL SAD
BUT YOU CAN.

YOU ARE CURRENTLY LOW ON ENERGY
BUT YOU CAN
PEOPLE WILL YOU TO, YOU CANNOT
BUT YOU CAN.
FOCUS ON WHAT YOU CAN
NOT WHAT YOU CANNOT.

LET YOUR INNER LIGHT SHINE
SHINE BRIGHTER THAN EVER
BE THAT LIGHTHOUSE.

IN THE TIMES OF DARKNESS
JUST AS YOU GO, TO GIVE IN
DO NOT
FOR THAT IS WHEN
INNER STRENGTH,
YOU NEVER KNEW YOU HAD, APPEARS.
YOU ARE NOT DISABLED
YOU JUST CANNOT DO WHAT THEY CAN

YOU ARE PERFECTLY IMPERFECT
YOU FIT IN, WHERE THEY CANNOT
YOU CAN DO WHAT THEY CANNOT.

WE ARE ALL DIFFERENT
WE ARE ALL UNIQUE IN OUR OWN SPECIAL WAY
STOP COMPARING, IT IS NOT A COMPETION
BE YOU, ACCEPT AND ACKNOWLEDGE YOU.

WITHOUT UNCONDITIONAL LOVE TOWARDS YOU
HOW CAN YOU UNCONDITIONALLY LOVE ANOTHER
UNCONDITIONAL LOVE DOES NOT MEAN
YOU PUT UP WITH THE MADNESS
OF OTHERS OR TOXICITY.

SIMPLY SEPARATE
HAVE PEACE BOTH ENDS
BEFORE YOU CAN LOVE SOMEONE ELSE
YOU GOT TO LOVE YOURSELF FIRST.

DROP THE EGO
BE HUMBLE
LOVE ONE ANOTHER
ONLY DO NOT FORGET YOU
LOVE
BE STRONG
SELF LOVE

A POETIC LETTER TO JOHNNY DEPP

THROUGH TIME AND SPACE
EINSTEIN ROSEN BRIDGE
MILKY WAYS TO GALAXY
COMA DIMENSIONS
CALL IT AS YOU WISH.

WELCOME TO THE WHIMSICAL WORLD
ANYTHING AND EVERYTHING IS POSSIBLE
WITH THE PSYCHOLOGY TO BELIEVE.

A NOD TO TIM BURTON
TILT OF A HAT
OOPS, ELECTROCUTED HAIR
CONCEPTION STEAM PUNK
CALLED JOHNNY DEPP.

CRAZY HAIR
SCISSORHANDS
HIGH TOP
MAD HATTER
ICHABOD CRANE GIZMO GADGETS
HOLLYWOOD VAMPIRE
WITH HIP CHAINS, KEYS AND SKULLS
STEAM PUNK NOT RUM PUNK.

A BUNCH OF STUFF

THAT IS ME TOO
WAREHOUSE TO WAREHOUSE
FUNNY YOU KNOW
I AM INSPIRED, I FEEL ALIVE.

THE TOOTH FAIRY
THE BUNNYMAN
SANTA CLAUS
DON'T FORGET JOHNNY DEPP.

I SHALL STOP TALKING MYSELF OUT
IF YOU MR DEPP STOP DOUBTING YOURSELF
LET'S NOT LIMIT OURSELVES
LET'S FACE IT
SOMEONE PAINTED A BLACK PICTURE WITH A
WHITE SQUARE IN THE MIDDLE
SOLD FOR £3,000,000.00
APPARENTLY, IT'S 'THE LIGHT AT
THE END OF THE TUNNEL'.

YOUR PASSION AND LOVE IS MUSIC
FOLLOWED CLOSELY BY PAINTING AND DRAWING
MAKING OTHERS LAUGH
PEOPLE MAY CALL YOU A FOOL
I SAY TO YOU 'WHAT A GOD GIVEN GIFT'.

THE LOVE AND PASSION YOU DEDICATE TOWARDS
EACH AND EVERY CHARACTER YOU PORTRAY
IS PURELY UNIQUE, AUTHENTIC
AND DARE I SAY AMAZING.

STAR DUST RUNS THROUGH YOUR VEINS
MR JOHNNY DEPP
WHEN YOU'RE SCARED, NERVOUS OR SHY
JUST REMEMBER YOU ARE CAPTAIN JACK SPARROW
FEARLESS INTO THE WILDERNESS.

YOU ARE WISER THAN YOU IMAGINE
I LISTEN TO YOU, I HEAR YOU
YOUR CONVERSATIONS AND THOSE CHAT SHOWS
LIFE EXPERIENCE IS KNOWLEDGE YOU KNOW....

WHO WOULD OF THOUGHT THE SHY, NERVOUS
MR JOHNNY DEPP, AUTHENTIC AND UNIQUE
WHO WEARS TANS AND MAKEUP
JUST TO BREATHE
BROUGHT SELF-ESTEEM AND CONFIDENCE TO ME.

SO, IN A SPIRITUAL WHIMISICAL WAY
YOU HELPED ME IN A UNIQUE WAY WITHOUT
KNOWING IT
THAT'S THE WHIMSICAL WAY.

SO, THANK YOU FOR THAT....
I LOST MY MUM LAST YEAR
THROUGH THE CHARACTERS YOU BRING TO LIFE
THE BEAUTIFUL 18 WITH MR JEFF BECK
YOU REVEALED A SOFTER SINGING VOICE.

MY GRIEVING WAS MADE EASIER
AND MORE WHIMSICAL
A PRECIOUS GIFT IS THAT
A BLESSING TO MY SOUL
AND FOR THAT I UNCONDITIONALLY LOVE YOU
IN A WHIMSICAL WAY.

AS BUDDY HOLLY WOULD SAY
POETRY IN MOTION
CONGRATULATIONS ON THAT BEATS
ACCOLADE HONOUR YOU GOT.

KIND REGARDS,

SHARON.

13 O'CLOCK

OH HOW BIZARRE
IT MUST BE THINKING THE CLOCK WAS ACCURATE
12 OR 24 HOURS A DAY.

HAVE YOU EVER STUDIED THE FACE
OF THE ROUND CLOCK?
NO MATTER WHAT THE TIME
ALWAYS EQUALS 13 O'CLOCK:
12 AND 1 MAKE 13
11 AND 2 MAKE 13
10 AND 3 MAKE 13
9 AND 4 MAKE 13
8 AND 5 MAKE 13
7 AND 6 MAKE 13
6 AND 7 MAKE 13
5 AND 8 MAKE 13
4 AND 9 MAKE 13
3 AND 10 MAKE 13
2 AND 11 MAKE 13
1 AND 12 MAKE 13.

OKAY
6 HOURS IN THE MORNING

6 HOURS IN THE AFTERNOON
6 HOURS BY NIGHT

WE ALL KNOW THERE'S 12 HOURS BY A.M
WE ALL KNOW THERE'S 12 HOURS BY P.M

24 HOURS IN A DAY
6 QUARTERLY BY 7 DAYS IN A WEEK
6 AND 7 MAKE 13.
OH LIKE, 'BAKERS DOZEN'.

TWICE A YEAR
CLOCKS SKIP AN HOUR
GOING FORWARD
GOING BACKWARDS
WHY'S THAT YOU ASK?

PRIVATE YOU KNOW
THE MAN IN THE MOON
BLOWS A KISS TO MOTHER EARTH
SHE SMILES RIGHT BACK
THE HOUR OF LOVE
BEES FLUTTERING
FOR THE 13TH HOUR IS KNOWN AS
THE HONEYMOON.

24 HOURS IN A DAY
DIVIDE BY 4 IS 6 QUARTERLY
7 DAYS IN A WEEK
6 AND 7 MAKES 13
THEREFORE ALWAYS 13 O'CLOCK!

THINK OF THE MAIDEN AND THE VIKING
DRINKING MEAD
GET IT?
13TH HOUR
THE HOUR OF LOVE!

LOVERS BLUSHERS MOON

OH LADY MOON
SHINE DOWN UPON THEE
MY LOVE IS AWAY
MAY IT BE BY SHIP AT SEA
OR ON A STAGE WITH A GUITAR
SOMEWHERE
KEEP HIM SAFE
KEEP HIM WARM
WITH YOUR LOVING ETERNAL PROTECTIVE LIGHT
GENTLE TO HIS SENSITIVE EYES
TELL HIM I LOVE HIM
WEAR SOME RED LIPSTICK
RED BLUSHER
AS HE LOVES HIS RED MOON.

* * *

I DON'T KNOW HERE I AM
I TRAVEL ALL AROUND
HERE, THERE AND EVERYWHERE
NOW LISTEN UP MR MOON
MY GIRL IS THERE,
WHILE I AM OVER HERE...
LOOK DOWN AT HER
LET ME KNOW SHE SAFE
AND MR MOON WHEN SHE LOOKS UP
DON'T FORGET TO GIVE A CHEEKY WINK.

PIRATES

WHEN IT IS DARK AND SCARY
CROSSROADS LEAD TO DEAD ENDS
EYES LOCKED INTO AN ABYSS
YOU FEEL LOST
THE MAP HAS INVISIBLE INK
NOWHERE TO RUN
ALONG COMES UNLIKELY HEROES
A PIRATE AND HIS SHIP MATE
JACK CAPTAIN WHITE WITH JOHNNY DEPP.

MEN OF MANY CHARACTERS
STRONG, BRAVE HOLDING THE HANDS
OF PARENTS WHO STARE INTO THE ABYSS
OF SICKNESS OF THEIR CHILD,
SAD, FRIGHTENED CHILDREN.
FOR A MOMENT IN TIME,
THEY ARE GIVEN HAPPINESS AND JOY.

THROUGH THE HUMOUR AND PLAY
WITH TWO ANGELIC PIRATES
BRINGING A SMILE AND A LIGHT
INTO A DARK DEPRESSING WORLD
WHERE MOST PEOPLE ARE SHY OR NERVOUS
AFRAID TO LOOK A FOOL OR OBSERVED BEING SILLY
JACK CAPTAIN WHITE AND HIS MATE JOHNNY DEPP.
IN THE FORM OF A PIRATE WHO FORGOT HIS NAME
A NAME THE WORLD KNOWS ALL OVER
CROSS BETWEEN A JACK IN THE BOX, A SPARROW

OH YES, CAPTAIN, I FORGOT
I DO BEG YOUR PARDON.

THESE MEN FACE THEIR ADVERSITY
WEARNING MAKE UP AND DRESSING
UP TO BRING A BIT OF SPARKLE
TO CHILDREN, ANIMALS AND ADULTS ALIKE.
SHOWING HUMANITY AND COMPASSION
INTO WHAT WOULD BE A TERRIFYING ORDEAL.
MAY IT BE A HOSPITAL OR A CHANCING MOMENT
ON THE STREET...
A HUG, A PHOTO, WITH A PIRATE
COME, RUN ALONG WITH JACK.

MY BELOVED MOTHER

I NEVER THOUGHT YOU WOULD EVER
PASS ON TO THE NEXT PLACE
OF SPIRIT'S JOURNEY
BEFORE ME.
I WOULD NOT BE ALIVE IF IT WAS NOT FOR YOU.
I DO NOT MEAN MY BIRTH.

MOTHER YOU REMAINED STEAD FAST
YOU WERE THERE FOR DAD
AS YOU BOTH WATCHED ME SLOWLY SLIP AWAY
NO ONE THOUGHT I SURVIVE THAT
MULIPLE ORGAN FAILURE.

YOU DID MOTHER.
EVEN WHEN THEY CALLED YOU BANANAS.
IT WAS NOT THE HOSPITAL; THEY RAN OUT OF IDEAS.
IT WAS YOU MOTHER
YOU BELIEVED I HAD TOO MUCH TO DO.

WHO WOULD HAVE, THOUGHT
COOKING SALT AND COWS PROTEIN COULD CREATE
A LIFE SHATTERING ALTERING CHALLENGE
THE TRINITY OF GOD, MOTHER AND DAUGHTER.
EVERY DAY YOU BELIEVE IN ME
YOU NEVER DOUBTED UNLIKE THE ENTIRE
WORLD WHEN I COULD NOT TALK, COULD NOT
BREATHE, COULD NOT EAT, COULD NOT WALK....
IN A COMA YOU STILL BELIVED.

I CALL IT MY STUBBORN STREAK
MOTHER, YOU SAID "MY DAUGHTER IS
DETERMINED TO SEE IT THROUGH"
THAT GIRL IS EMPATHIC AND I KNOW SHE KNOWS.

MY BELOVED MOTHER YOU ARE
NEVER GONE FROM ME
YOU KNOW I KNOW THE SOUL SPIRIT LIVES ON
I FEEL YOUR ENERGY SURROUNDING
ME IN A BLANKET OF FOG,
OF LOVE, COMFORT AND PEACE.

MOTHER YOU ALWAYS SAID,
WHEN THE RIGHT TIME COMES ALONG.
THE RIGHT ONE FOR ME,
WILL FIND ME.
WELL, HE DID

MOTHER YOU ARE MY ROCK, EVEN IF YOU CALLED ME
'THE FAMILY ROCK'
AS I KEPT YOU AND DAD STRONG.
I CANNOT EVER BE AS STRONG AS YOU ARE.

I AM FAR TOO SENSITIVE, BUT I, GUESS I
GOT STRENGTH IN OTHER WAYS TO.
WE ARE INSEPARABLE MOTHER.
NOW YOUR FREE FROM FLESH
NO MORE SUFFERING OR PHYSICAL PAIN
OUR SOULS AND SPIRIT ETERNALLY ENTWINNED.

I LOVE YOU MY BELOVED MOTHER!

DAD

NOW, WHERE WOULD I BE
WITHOUT MY DAD?
A GENLTLE, TENDER, QUIET MAN
WHO I LOVE WITH ALL MY HEART
JUST AS I DID AND DO MY BELOVED MOTHER.

MY DAD IS TRULY UNIQUE
THERE IS NO OTHER RATHER LIKE MY DAD
HE ALWAYS SAID: "GO ASK YOUR MUM",
NOW MUM HAS PASSED AWAY TO THE NEXT PLACE.
NOW DAD MUST ASK HIMSELF....
WILL A HUG DO....
THAT'S WHAT I CAN DO
DADS LIKE MINE ARE BLESSED WITH HUMOUR
THE ANSWERS AND ADVICE FROM MUM
WELL, AS DAD SAYS: "WHAT WOULD SHE SAY?"
I WAS EVEN MUM'S ROCK
OR WAS THAT MY COOKING!
IT MOST DEFINITELY WAS NOT YOURS DAD.

SHERRI PIE

IF YOU ARE ALL COLD AND ALONE
RAINED ON
SNOWED ON
BURST WATER PIPE ON
MICROWAVE BROKEN DOWN ON
YOUR WASHING MACHINE GOT HICCUPS
BROKEN HEARTED
DON'T FEEL WELL.

DON'T DESPAIR
THERE IS ALWAYS THE MAN OF STEELE
TOO TRUE, TOO LOUD, ELECTRIC GUITARS
NOT FOR A COLD, BROKEN HEARTED MIGRAINE.

WOOSH GOES THE WIND
DO NOT FEAR THAT JUST O' CHEERY WILLOW
PLAYING AROUD THE WILLOW
TREE AT THE BRIT GARDEN
BIG HUG PASSING BY THROUGH THE
HOUSE RUNNING TO THE TREE...
GOT YOU IN A SPIN.

I KNOW WHAT YOU NEED....
A CUP OF COFFEE, CHOCOLATE CAKE
AIR FRIED COOKED MEAL
COSY COUCH WITH A GREAT HUG
BIG FLUFFY CARDIGAN.
A SHOULDER TO LEAN ON

EARS THAT HEAR
WARM SMELL OF PIE
NUMBER ONE BODYGUARD
STRONG STUFF DON'T MESS WITH SHERRI PIE
SHE PART STEELE AND PART BARBE WIRE
SWEETENED WITH AMARETTO....

LOVE ETERNAL

DID YOU KNOW LOVE AND HATE
ARE NOT TO THE BODY
BUT A STATE OF MIND, THAT'S THE SPIRIT YOU KNOW.
YOUR PERSONALITY AND CHARACTER ARE A STATE
PERPLEX COMPLEX SPIRIT
A SOUL IF YOU PREFER.

DEATH IS NATURE COMES TO US ALL
WHETHER IT BE IN YOUR SLEEP
A DISEASE LIKE CANCER
OR A WOUND TO THE BODY FRAGILE.

THERE IS MORE TO THE SPIRIT OR
SOUL THAN ONE BELIEVES
IS IT A MYTH, A FANTASY OR BLIND IGNORANCE?
WHY ALL ANGELS NOW
SOUL AND SPIRT NEVER DIES.

THERE IS SPIRITUAL LIFE AFTER DEATH.

LOOK THROUGHOUT HISTORY
PEOPLE WILL KNOW, FOLK TALES, YOU KNOW.
THE TELEVISION WILL SAY
'FOR ENERTAINMENT PURPOSES ONLY'
SO, THEY SAY.

SPIRITS WERE BORN OUT OF LOVE
CREATED LIKE A BABY

SOME TO HELP
SOME TO DESTROY.

HEARTBREAKING HISTORY, THROUGHTOUT TIME
HOW SOME NEGATIVE FORCE CREATED POLITICS
TO TURN HUMANS TO HATE
OR
TO DESTROY BY ORDER TO BE KILLED.

HOW SAD, HOW TERRIFYING IT MUST BE.
A FARMER, A FISHER OR EVEN SOLIDER
WITH JUST HAY PITCH FORKS, GIVEN A MUSKET, A
LANCE A PISTOL FORCED BY POLITICS AND YOU DIE.

FIFTY, A HUNDRED, SEVERAL HUNDRED YEARS
EVEN A THOUSAND YEARS NOT
KNOWING YOU ARE DEAD.
THE WRONG PLACE, WRONG TIME, WRONG PERSON
HANGED FOR A CRIME THEY NEVER DID.

IS IT HAUNTING OR A CRY FOR HELP
TOWARDS SENSES THAT ARE BLIND
OR DEAF TO THE SIXTH SENSE.
THAT'S THE CRY OF LOST SOUL.

UNLIKEY WARRIORS CALLED CHRIS AND IAN
WITH THEIR TRUSTED SIDE KICKS RYAN AND BARRI
COME TO THE RESCUE OF THE UNKNOWN TO THE
LIVING SURROUNDED BY MISUNDERSTANDINGS.

IS IT A POLTERGEIST? PROBABLY.
LIKE A TODDLER ACCIDENTALLY LOCKED IN A ROOM.

HELP, HELP, BANG, BANG.
OH DEAR, NOBODY HEARS.

WITH HIS GADGETS OF TECHNOLOGY
THE BRAVE KNIGHT RYAN SEEKS OUT
"WAS IT YOU?"
ANOTHER ROOM
BARRI "AHHHHHHH WHAT THE HECK?"
RYAN SPEAKS OUT
"OKEY, DID I MISS SOMETHING?"

STOP, DON'T MOVE
SOMEONE OR SOMETHING IN THERE
A SPIRIT, AN ELEMENTAL OR AN ALIEN WHO KNOWS?
SECURITY CHECK FOR INTRUDERS....

IN COMES EMPATHY, SENSATIONS OF THE BODY
REACTING TO VIBRATIONS PICKED UP.
BY THE SOUL.
ANOTHER SPIRIT IS NEAR

*****NOTE FROM THE AUTHOR:
THIS POEM IS DEDICATED TO IAN LAWMAN AND
BARRI GHAI (HELP! MY HOUSE IS HAUNTED).
NOT FORGETTING CHRIS FLEMMING AND RYAN O'NEILL
(HAUNTED/SPOOKED IRELAND & HAUNTED
SCOTLAND/SPOOKED SCOTLAND).

(THIS POEM IS ESPECIALLY DEDICATED
TO MEDIUM CHRIS FLEMING,
MAY THE GOOD LORD CONTINUE TO HELP
YOU FIGHT YOUR CANCER BATTLE)

LOVE LIVES ON

WHO GOES THERE?
I HEAR YOU? I FEEL YOU?
WHAT'S YOUR NAME? MY NAME
IS CHRIS WHAT'S YOURS?

THIS IS NOT RESIDUAL IT'S
INTELLIGENT LIFE OF ITS OWN
QUESTION IS ELEMENTAL, ALIEN OR SPIRIT?
PAST OR FUTURE?
AHA, YOU THOUGHT YOU MUST BE
A PAST LIFE TO BE A SPIRIT....

GUESS AGAIN FOLKS
SOMETIMES THE FUTURE HAUNTS
JUST LIKE THE PAST
A GLIMPSE IN TIME
A WOBBLE IN THE UNIVERSE

OH, I SEE, THE CAT CAUGHT YOUR TONGUE.

SPIRITS ARE ALL AROUND YOU
BUT WHAT YOU SEE –
ARE THE LIVING CALLED 'YOU AND
ME' THE FLESH WORLD.
WHAT'S ALL THE RACKET FOR?
TELL ME YOUR STORY
HOW CAN I HELP?

I CAN HEAR YOU....
OTHERS CANNOT, THEY NOT WITH THE GIFT.
RYAN, PASS ME THAT PLEASE?
PUT THE SPEAKER ON
IT'S OKAY, NO NEED TO BE AFRAID....
CHRIS, YOU HEAR THAT MATE?

"MASS"
"PRIEST"
"GOD"
HOW DO YOU DIE?
"FIRE"
"DEFENDING CASTLE, INVADERS SET ALIGHT"

HOW OLD ARE YOU?
"12"
WHY THE INVASION?
"ROBERT DE BRUCE FIGHTS EDWARD OF ENGLAND"
RYAN IS THAT WILLIAM WALLACE TIME?
AYE CHRIS, IT IS.
"CAN'T FIND MY MOTHER OR FATHER".
WITH A GENTLE VOICE
CHRIS CALLS FOR ARCHANGEL
MICHAEL AND THE ANGELS

TO CLEAR AWAY ANY NEGATIVE ENERGIES....
CALLS TO THE LORD AND TO THE FATHER, GOD
TO BRING FORTH THE LIGHT....
CHRIS SAYS A PRAYER SO THE
SPIRITS CAN RETURN HOME.

TO THE LORD
RETURN TO LOVE....
TIRED, WEARY CHRIS FLEMING
SHOWS UNCONDITIONAL LOVE
LOVE TO ALL, FOR ONE DAY.

YOU TOO COULD BE A SPIRIT WITHOUT
FLESH NEEDING HELP TOO!

SO, YOU SEE LOVE LIVES ON AFTER THE FLESH IS GONE!

THE GREAT MIRACLE AND THE GREAT SIN OF NOTRE DAME

THE WORLD IN CHAOS AND GREAT TURMOIL
WOE TO THE PEOPLE
IT TOOK AN ACT OF GOD TO WAKE THEM UP
A MYSTERIOUS MIRACULOUS FIRE BREAKS
OUT ONLY DESTROYING WHAT IS WOOD.

NO MELTING OF GREAT ORGAN PIPES
NO DAMAGE TO THE WOODEN CROSS
NO DAMAGE TO THE MARBLE STONES
LIMESTONE DID NOT MELT
JUST FELL AND SMASHED UPON THE FLOOR.

IT TOOK A TEAM OF JESUS OF
NAZARETH – THE CARPENTER
LIKE IS HUMAN STEP-FATHER JOSEPH
TO REBUILD IT, FROM OAK TREES
FALLEN FROM FRANCE
THAT IS OKAY, AS WE KNOW A
TRESS DISEASE IS KILLING
THE EARTH'S OAK TREES.

THE LESSON AND MIRACLE HERE -
IS THAT PEOPLE CAME TOGETHER
SHOWING UNCONDITIONAL LOVE

WOE TO THE CITY
SUCH A GREAT SIN
COULD HAVE REBUILT AROUND THE ALTER
MARBLE STATUES OF NOTRE DAME CATHEDRAL
USING CHEAPER WAYS.

VOLUNTARY WORK OFFERED TO GOD
WHY USE 850 MILLION EUROS ON A BUILDING?
I AM SURE PEOPLE WOULD HAVE
DONATED TO GOD FREELY
MATERIALS AND THE TIME THEY GOT
COULD HAVE BEEN DONE WITH 100 MILLION EUROS....

WOE TO THE CITY
STARVING FARMERS OUT
NO FARMERS – NO BLOOMING FOOD
NO FOOD
NO FOOD – NO PEOPLE.

ALL GONE TO HEAVEN
YIKES!
850 MILLION EUROS USED
NO MORE FOOD, NO MORE PEOPLE
NO MORE WORKPLACE OF COMMERCE
YIKES!
CITY OF PARIS KILLED OF TAX!!!
THE GREAT MIRACLE AND THE
GREAT SIN OF NOTRE DAME.

ATTRACTION AND LOVE

OH, WHAT A SMILE
IT LIGHTS UP MY WORLD
WHAT A GIGGLE CRACKS ME UP
SO WISE
SO YOUTHFUL
ALWAYS KNOWS WHAT TO DO
IT ATTRACTS....

A SUDDEN SITUATION
SMILES GOES UPSIDE DOWN
GIGGLES TURNS TO TEARS
WISDOM BECOMES IGNORANCE
HAS NO CLUE WHAT TO DO
WHY TURN TO ME?
IT'S A TURN OFF....

IF I IGNORE IT, IT SORTS ITSELF OUT
THAT'S ATTRACTION
AS LOVE HELPS AND OFFERS SUPPORT
LOVE SEES IT AS AN HONOUR
WHEN LOVE RUNS TO THEM FOR HELP OR ADVICE
THERE IS A BIG DIFFERENCE TO THAT
'LIKING' OR 'LOVING'
'STRENGTH VS WEAKNESSES'.

ABOUT THE AUTHOR

Sharon Downey was born in London, England. Where she lives with her Father. This book is in dedication to her late mother. Sharon has always had a passion for poetry as, well as music. Whilst she studied at secondary school she enjoyed Wordsworth, Shelley and Byron and as well as William Shakespeare.

ABOUT THE BOOK

DIVERSE means "Different; unlike; various".

LOVE means "To regard with affection; to like; to delight in".

There are many ways a person can have love. Love can be platonic, romantic or passionate. Love can be joy and pain, sorrow as well as happiness.

Words form a fan:

"I have been reading Sharon's poetry on Facebook for three years now.

I do tell her; she has got talent here. I do thank her for the poem 'Sherri Pie' that I so love. She is unique with her own style. It is very refreshing.

I wish her luck and encouragement with revised edition and re-launch of 'Diverse Love'."

~ Sherri. L. Steele *(Maryland, USA)*

* 9 7 8 1 9 6 7 3 6 1 7 9 3 *